Science Vocabulary Readers

The Earth

Megan Duhamel

SCHOLASTIC INC.

NEW YORK • TORONTO • LONDON • AUCKLAND • SYDNEY
MEXICO CITY • NEW DELHI • HONG KONG • BUENOS AIRES

ISBN-13: 978-0-545-00731-3 / ISBN-10: 0-545-00731-3

Photos Credits:
Cover: © Bryan Allen/Corbis; title page: © Roger Harris/Photo Researchers; contents page, from top: © Comstock/Corbis, © The Stock Connection/Punchstock, © David Muench/Getty Images; page 4: © Comstock/Corbis; page 5: © Peter Turner/Getty Images; page 6: © Bryan Allen/Corbis; page 7, top left: © Frank Siteman/Getty Images; page 7, top right: © James Warwick/Getty Images; page 7, bottom left: © David Noton/Getty Images; page 7, bottom right: © Martin Ruegner/Getty Images; page 8: © Lefty's Editorial Services/Jim McMahon; page 9: © Stock Connection/Punchstock; page 10: © John Burcham/ Getty Images; page 10, inset: © Lefty's Editorial Services/Jim McMahon; page 11: © Flying Colours LTD/ Getty Images; page 11, inset: © Lefty's Editorial Services/Jim McMahon; page 12: © David Muench/Getty Images; page 13: © Digital Vision/Getty Images; page 14: © Perry Mastrovito/Corbis; page 15: © David Sutherland/Getty Images; page 16: © Bryan Allen/Corbis; back cover: © Stockbyte/Getty Images RF.

Photo research by Dwayne Howard
Design by Holly Grundon

Copyright © 2007 by Lefty's Editorial Services
All rights reserved. Published by Scholastic Inc.

12 11 10 9 8 7 6 5   9 10 11 12/0

Printed in the U.S.A.
First printing, December 2007

Contents

Chapter 1

What Is the Earth?

Where are you right now? You may be in your home. You may be at school. But wherever you are, you are on the Earth.

Fast Fact

The Earth is more than four billion years old.

The Earth is a planet. The Earth is round. The Earth is beautiful! It looks like a blue marble from far away.

water   **United States**

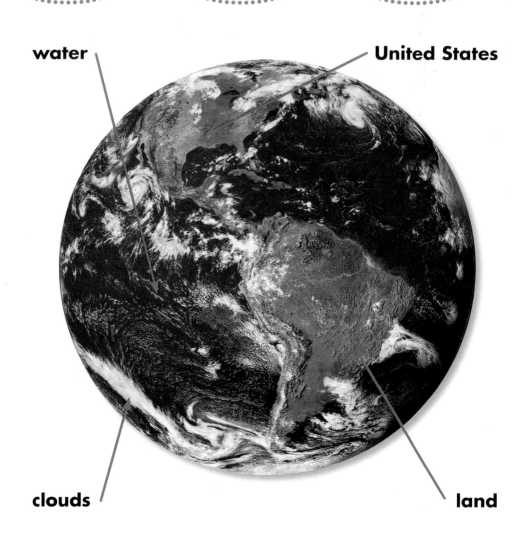

clouds   **land**

Most of the Earth is covered with water. But there is also a lot of land. Take a close look. You can see the United States!

girl

lion

All of these living things breathe air.

flower

tree

The Earth is surrounded by a thick blanket of air called the **atmosphere**. Plants and animals all breathe this air. The Earth is the only planet where living things have been found.

Chapter 2

The Moving Earth

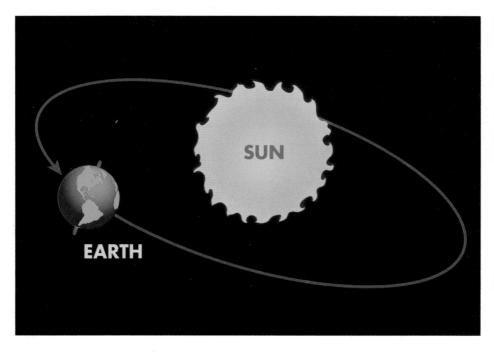

The Earth revolves around the sun.

You cannot feel it, but the Earth is always moving. It travels around the sun on an invisible path. It takes about one year to go all the way around.

It is day here.

SUN

EARTH

It is night here.

The Earth rotates as it moves around the sun.

The Earth spins like a top as it travels around the sun. When one part of the Earth faces the sun, another part faces away. That is why we have days and nights.

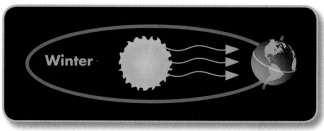

Winter

Why do we have seasons? The Earth is tilted as it moves around the sun. When the part of Earth with the United States is tilted away from the sun like this, it is winter. Brrrr!

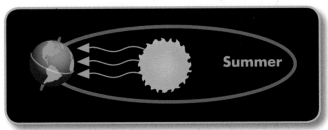

Summer

When the part of Earth with the United States is tilted toward the sun like this, it is summer. We get hotter weather because more of the sun's **rays** reach us. We also get more hours of sunlight.

Chapter 3

The Changing Earth

Grand Canyon

The Earth is always changing. Wind and water carve deep **canyons**. It took millions of years to make the Grand Canyon.

Fast Fact

Lava comes from deep inside the Earth.

Lava flows from volcanoes. The lava cools and hardens. This can build tall mountains.

New York City

People also change the Earth. They build farms. They build towns. They build big cities.

Fast Fact

More than six-and-a-half billion people inhabit the Earth.

We must always take good care of the Earth. It is our own special home in space!

Glossary

atmosphere (**at**-muhss-fihr): the blanket of air that surrounds the Earth

canyon (**kan**-yuhn): a deep, narrow river valley with steep sides

inhabit (in-**hab**-it): to live in a place

lava (**lah**-vuh): the hot liquid rock that pours out of a volcano

ray (**ray**): a beam of light from the sun

revolve (ri-**volv**): to keep turning in a circle around an object

rotate (**roh**-tate): to spin around or turn like a wheel

Comprehension Questions

1. Can you explain how the Earth moves?

2. Can you explain how the Earth changes?

3. Can you think of four excellent words to describe the Earth?